Copyright © 2024 Beautiful Heart LLC All rights reserved

No part of this book may be reproduced, or stored in a retrieval system, or transmitted in any form or by any means, electronic, mechanical, photocopying, recording, or otherwise, without express written permission of the publisher.

Love Is My Shelter

By

Ayesha Montgomery

Introduction — 6
Prologue — 8
Part 1 — 9
Higher — 9
- Barriers — 10
- Rays of Sunshine on the Roof — 11
- Connection — 12
- Ways — 13
- Good Time Sally — 15
- Running The Race — 16
- Love and Indifference — 20
- Miss Each Other — 22
- Status: Complicated — 23
- Rough Tides — 25
- Warm Sand — 27
- Long Ago Love — 28
- Lack of Trying — 29
- The Edge of Romance — 31
- Waiting — 33

Part 2 — 34
Life is Complicated — 34
- Ugly Truth — 35
- Still Living — 37
- Deceitful — 39
- Girl Child — 42
- Removed From Facebook — 45
- Silence — 51
- A Poem About Mourning — 54
- Forgiveness — 56
- Monster — 57
- Rise and Fall — 59
- Cookout — 60
- Ice Numbs It — 61

Yet to See	62
Never the Same	65
Restless	67
Rewind	68
Part 3	70
Feed The Soul	70
People	71
In Your Shell	74
Lighthouse	75
Pools	77
Missing Rubber Bands	79
Stronger	81
Lust	82
Love	83
Evening	84
Missing you	85
The Past	86
Ode to Laughter	87
What About Love?	88
Dust	89
Someone Else	90
Never Apart	91
Something Different	92
Part 4	96
Happiness in Transition	96
Speak	97
Profit	98
Able to Find	100
Telephone	102
Sweltering Heat	103
Much Needed Rest	104
Late Bloomer	106
Skin	108
Descent	111

Rock Steady	112
Love Jones	113
Travel With Hope	116
Eagle	118
Think of You	119
Lasting Love	121
Carefully Made Home	122
My Truth	123
Material World	126
New Beginnings	128
A Few Words for the Road	130

Introduction

The process of writing *Love Is My Shelter* brought me to my knees. I started writing this book in 2021 and I finished writing it the same year. A few months later, my Father died, nearly 6 months later my Auntie died then 3 months later my Grandmother died. I decided to continue working on the book as a result. These poems are exposing a more vulnerable side of me that I normally don't share with people. I remember telling my uncle that I cried all the time since the passing of my Father and he refused to believe me. It was crazy! I realized that sometimes I'm so shut off emotionally that people think I'm stronger than I am. But experiencing so many deaths in a short period of time truly shook me to the core. It was the most painful experience of my life. As a result, my family strife became more pronounced and my internal and spiritual battle intensified. *Love is My Shelter* helped me work things out mentally and spiritually. This book was birthed out of tragedy and heartbreak but it's still hopeful. While my life was falling apart, I didn't realize Christ was putting the pieces together for me. My hope is that this book will inspire people that are on the edge of giving up. The same way that writing it helped me. Thank you for reading.

Prologue

Writing is a nasty business. One minute you're speaking with your whole heart. Baring the issues of your soul on a white paper that seems endless. The next minute your words dry up like a shallow puddle of water on a hot summer's day. The words fade to black and the feeling of flowing letters pulsating through easy fingertips slips away. We sit with open palms writing for the pleasure of the moment, praying for the eyes of excited readers to scan the lines of tactful words. We are not titans. We are bearers of empty yet hopeful words, subjects added to verbs. Creating sentences you never thought of but every portion read touched a sensitive nerve. We fly like oceans sweeping over wet dreams. We move like clouds rolling too high. Fighting for an opening to a sentence. Working towards a period that never dies. People have limited lives but the feelings they provoke live on. Count me among the nameless writers who gave up but kept on going. Never knowing if anyone would read. Because they couldn't change the world and success is defined by monetary greed. But the starving artist is defined by need.

Part 1

<u>Higher</u>

There you are
Intriguing with your lips
Just verbs, nouns and verses
Strung together like stars in a limitless sky
Your love takes an anxious heart
Higher and higher

Barriers

You were made to cross powerful rivers
The tide will quell at your feet
Your chill will extinguish a volcano
In the mist of erupting
The wind of your hand will silence the rumbling giant
Your smile will break barriers
That bar your entrance
Doors will swing open when you turn about face
You are special with a presence that can't be replaced
So when you are being challenged
Move like you already won the race!

Rays of Sunshine on the Roof

The hard fought wars
Are internal
Ego, guilt and shame
Never dealing with hurt

Praying the next relationship won't be the same
Many tender hearts are losing
In this game
Of love and war

I want a love
That holds me at the waist
And narrows at my feet
But knows how to be discreet

Something that feels special
Because our connection is unique
I want a love that loves me out loud
But is silent about our intimacy

Connection

It's the conversation for me
The words, thoughts and phrases
Exchanged between traveling moments
And liberated souls

Akin to cold lemonade
On a summer's day
Making the discussions
Go from morning into the warm night

Giving power to easy smiles
And playful jokes
Enabling people to exist
Encouraging the hopeful to emote
It's the conversation for me

Ways

How to address
A heart rubbed sore?
It is too raw to touch
Red, purple and blue
Cover a surface that once desired you

This puzzle is fragmented
Into a 1000 pieces of complicated moments
Missed opportunities
Near kisses and brief hugs
We love to mourn, groan
And long for love

Restore the dream
Look past the surface
In search of the core
Always dancing in step
But begging for more
Hands ache to touch
Eyes dare to explore

Where are the edges of a jagged heart?
Do they lead to the seashore?
Will the current make the rough corners smooth?
Are they solitary or do they move?

What happens to a soul
That lost hope too soon?
Does it shake like a leaf on a tree branch?
Blown by turbulent skies?

Daring to look for friendship
In the same place where love died
To extinguish and rekindle an orange flame that burns
Darker than red wine

If the passing of time is tender
Let the hand of God be kind
Arranging purpose and patterns
That man is unable to design

We ease into circumstance
Reaching out for feelings
That roar like a lion in search of his pride
For what is a king without a queen?
A groom without a bride
So we look for ways to address it

Good Time Sally

Cherish your loved ones while you can
Kiss their rosy cheeks
Hold their precious hand
Speak uplifting words in their moments of tribulation

Pray with them
Let them know that you can sympathize
Show warmth to express
That you understand

When the wind beats at their worn door
Stand beside them as a friend
The things that we forget we did
Mean something in the end

So cherish your loved ones while you can
Give them wild flowers
And provide them with hope
That a tired heart can comprehend
Because no one wants to be alone

When the hard days come
The good time Sally and John are cool
Until the lightning strikes
It's those moments when you want a caring soul
To make sure you're alright

Running The Race

See we just sinners
Saved by grace
So I praise God a thousand different ways
No matter the challenges I face
Even if my attempts for a better life
Blow up in my face

The test leads to a testimony that man can't erase
Pushing past the competition
Like a track star that ran a long race
But I'm only competing with myself
Refusing to bow down for money, sex appeal or wealth
The cost is too high

I seen girl's sell their body fresh out of college
While reaching for the sky
Cause the bachelor's degree wasn't paying without experience
And experience only paid minimum wage

So for the money she was a kitten
For green she became a slave
The loans wore her down
But the pills made her behave
Yet I still see the beauty in her countenance
The cold streets never iced her soul

Many of us have been through unspoken hell
But our hearts still shine like gold
Polish it and ignore the lies that your told
There are no easy paths to freedom

People try to look down on others
To gain a sense of control

Fighting with the demons
That spoke ill things to them
Since they were 3 years old
But that's alright though
Whatever folks gotta do to sleep at night though
Anything to camouflage the remnants of a broken soul

Some people got the game messed up
So I tell them keep your head up
Even when the fire is roaring like an angry lion
Never let up
Cause the best comes
When your in-between a rock and a hard place
When no place is a safe space

See we just sinners
Saved by grace
So I praise God a thousand different ways
No matter the challenges I face
Even if my attempts for a better life
Blow up in my face

I filled out the applications on indeed
My resume is like a haggard boulevard it goes on for miles
I work till I quit like it's going out of style
I'm in my 30s beating the streets like a juvenile
With no bed time

Paying to live but still catching fines

Avoiding crows feet like a queen in my prime
So when people talk to me
It's hard to deny that Jesus is working overtime

Keeping my skin tight
And my smile bright
So even in the blanket of night I shine
Cause people can't stop what's devine
With only 5 dollars in my pocket
I'm still a dime

And my faith is the base of icy rhymes
So when I'm done chilling
I'm blessed in God's time
I remember the smell of smoke in the air
With no haze, eyes and hands cocked with no glaze

See we just sinners
Saved by grace
So I praise God a thousand different ways
No matter the challenges I face
Even if my attempts for a better life
Blow up in my face

Cause I had some shots fired in my direction
Hollow clips aiming for abdomens near the intersection
Killer intent paid short term bills
But ignored the cost of rent

Our time here is temporary
I hope mine is well spent
See I understand the fight

But Able's blood cries from the ground
Because of his brother's internal strife

Can you use the master's tools to dismantle his house?
Trying to build something new
But the same result comes out
A new fence and porch, painted red
All over jealousy and spoiled bread
How can a desperate soul get ahead?

See I'm just a sinner
Saved by grace
So I praise God a thousand different ways
No matter the challenges I face
Even if my attempts for a better life
Blow up in my face

Love and Indifference

Pray with me because it's getting really crazy out here
I hear gunshots on my block everyday
Police barcade the street at least 3 times a week
Around my way a 14 year old caught 2 bullets to the chest
All he wanted was some juju beans from the gas station

Now he's in intensive care
His Mom cries for the child that's barely a teen
The news covers the scene but forgets the person
Nevertheless, the reality isn't changing
The father is nowhere to be found

The community is complacent
I bet you the shooter will walk
In the hood we speak
But the real ones don't talk,
Words fall to the broken concrete

And weeds spring from the blood and tears of unrealized hope
We laugh to smile, we smile to cope in the wake of hard days
And complicated situations…
There is beauty still

Throw some food on the barbeque,
A tender soul is in need of a good time
We nourish the needy round here
We tend to our sick

Give respect to the elderly and mow their lawns free of charge
Where happiness is genuine and love is hard to find

In spite of it all, we have peace
And the world can't take it because God gave it

Little MoMo an em' shoot dice
And chop it up for days on end
Knowing pain comes with the tide
But this feeling of comfort can't be swept away

Because you can only understand high when you've touched low
Love is personified through the understanding of hate
Heat is applied through pressure
Acceptance can only be felt through the lens of rejection

There is no battle that you can't overcome
The struggle has been fought
And the battle has been won,
You are the rose that grew in the hood

There are few people
Who wouldn't succumb
To the hurt you endured
So keep pushing

You are the green grass
That creates foliage in the heart of men
You are hope ever growing
In a landscape coated in love and indifference
Watered by the dreams of your forefathers
You are the bedrock of sweet dreams to me

Miss Each Other

It seems like we always
Manage to miss each other
Getting close
But never close enough

Desiring a kiss
Longing for a touch
But always a stone's throw away
Awaiting tomorrow to embark
On the feeling of love we have today

Planning for a future
We have yet to see
And hoping tender feelings
Are here to stay

Status: Complicated

We've gone through so many phrases…
Of caring
Then not caring
Then caring again

Are we even lovers?
Can we ever be friends?
But for some reason
We think of each other often

So I guess that makes us complicated
You want things simple
But I leave you frustrated
And although we both hate it
We always look back

What you up to big head?
Baby where you at?
It's good to hear from you
Every now and then
But don't let my imagination get to wandering

Because I never left
I just needed time alone
I just wanted time to myself
Long enough to realize that I missed you

Counting down the hours, minutes and seconds
Until I would be greeted by the pearly whites
Of your radiant smile
Meet me here at our favorite spot

Between the phrases and empty spaces
Of a love too good to forget

Rough Tides

To burn the midnight oil
Looking for a peaceful space in a turbulent world
Many nights have passed by restless eyelids that refuse to close
Windows with open drapes peer into a restless soul

We will dance on a ballroom floor
Made from the dust and gravel of a broken time
A sea full of glass and broken bottles
That once carried hopeful wishes to shore…
Beacons me.

Desiring a life devoid of maybes
How much longer can a full heart wait?
Not stirred by longing, untouched by faith?
We once sailed these rough tides together

The uneven edges of your smile was my swan song
I squeezed your arm
Played in the crevices of your disbelief
Hung on to every word as though it were a testimony

We made memories here!
Standing under moonlit skies
Talking about future plans that never came into fruition
Holding on to fragile desires that fall from shaking, unstable hands

Once upon a time, I called you my man
We danced on tightropes, talked without words
And hated the space we shared
Our relationship was bad
Yet and still we made memories here

We will meet each other at the base of restless eyes
Long drawn out plans
The serenade of crickets
Chirping in a hopeful land

It is here that we will dance
On the dust and gravel of bliss times
To believe in the dream
Sore eyelids left behind

Warm Sand

We can't live forever
Treasure our time together
Sweet talk for days
Kiss the blues away

Allow glittering lights to shine
Like dew dropping off emerald leaves
In the springtime
Walk on the warm, hot sand

Let loose toes dig into fragmented glass
It glitters like sunshine on the edge
Of a new dream
We look toward the horizon

Smiling with the glow of happiness rising
Grasp dainty wrists
Then hold open hands
Let love be your anchor in the shoreline
Where we stand
This is the beauty of discovering love again

Long Ago Love

Long long ago
Love lived here
It thrived in the hope
Of fresh dreams

It grew
In the depths of moist moss
Moving with the wind
Clinging to the back of swift horses

Hoping for a moment
That expands beyond
The reach of always
Love that gave meaning

To the breath of a new day
Feelings that create more feelings
That are bound to stay
Attaching itself to open ends

And steady hearts
Eager to be filled with something more
Than disappointing fantasies
That fall flat like soda

Left open two days too long
The taste no longer satisfies
The pallet
Looking for a sensation
That is long gone

Lack of Trying

On gray days
When sun rays can't seem to reach me
I get sad from a lack of trying
Then denying
And whining

As I hear the call of my ambitions
Echoing through the distance
My pride responds back,
I'm tired, I can't do that
It's too hard, it'll never work
If I try, I will fall
If I skin my knee, it will hurt

I gotta put me first
Even if I wrap myself in a blanket
Of self pity that fails to break my fall
I done been up and down in my life
And this here… Ain't living at all

I'm wound too tight
If a line has too much tension
The fish won't bite
But if I never go to bank
Too afraid of the overcast
My spirit will die

My pride responds back,
I'm tired, I can't do that
It's too hard, it'll never work
If I try, I will fall

If I skin my knee it will hurt

Because I won't deal with the inside
Running from the insight on the things
That make me hide
Encouraging me to crumble instead of fight

Giving me reason to cling
To the embrace of an empty life
Empowering me to ignore
The torment of the day

But this is my season
The pink velvety rose takes in shimmering sunshine
Waiting to be pollinated by traveling bees
Sporting buzzers and patience
To touch the dream

The Edge of Romance

What does a punch drunk heart know about love?
It feels without remorse
It beats without a care
Calm when you're around
Then on edge when your not there
One minute up

The next down
A tryst comes
Romance goes
But the connection stays the same
Bathing in the sunshine

Soaking in the warmth of the rain
Trying against all odds
Racking the memories of a battered brain
Praying non stop
Till your lips run out of words to say

Believing all night
Questioning all day
Wondering why old love fails to fade
It follows you through adulthood

It holds you close through old age
Like a vintage bottle of wine
The taste grows more robust and crisp with time
Turning into a flavor that's too complex to define
What does a punch drunk heart know about love?

It feels without remorse

It beats without a care
Calm when you're around
Then on edge when your not there

It roams like a hermit crab devoid of a shell
Wandering for acceptance
Looking for a peaceful place to dwell
Knowing that happiness is a hop, skip and jump away

But rarely getting over the hill
Even though it's given up
It's excited still
And that's the nature of bruises
They're made to heal

Waiting

Restless hearts want to know…
How far does your love go?
Does it swing to the bedrock of a damp soul?
Or does it soar like an eagle in mid-flight?

Does it vanish during the day?
Then exhume at night?
Is it the peak of hope?
Or the plains in-between?

Could it be the moment when thoughts become feelings?
Or is it the brilliance found in every second of anticipation?
It's the dire need built up by waiting
It's the feeling of running without fainting

Part 2

<u>Life is Complicated</u>

I thought I was powerful till I met God
And I thought I knew evil
But then I met the devil

Ugly Truth

I've been writing for a real long time
But I feel like folks can't hear me
Because whenever stuff gets real people get scary
They're looking for the comfort in tales I can't provide
So they go to another person for their supply
That stuff hurt me a couple times
I can't even lie

Maybe this poetry doesn't mean anything
If these words fall flat
Then I'm just a fool holding onto foolish hope
Fasting from over a decade of lustful living
So my heart can cope

How to bare the rising sun
Without the use of men or weed?
Temptation calls my name like it misses me
And my flesh misses it
The spirit is well versed
But my mind is ill equipped

Like jack poured over ice with no chaser
I prefer brown liquor straight
And if I don't feel like talking
I'd rather have sex than pretend to date
That's how absent turns to hate
High expectations meeting a realistic fate

But there's so much love in me
And there was a time when my soul longed for company
I was born to a former Mac, player and hustler

So I was born with that rough love embedded in me

Ain't never felt the need to lie to men
The truth speaks with and without words
It's simple to comprehend
I don't run around the rosemary bush

When I utter words
Acknowledgement fills the room
But I gave just as good as I got
I recall my middle school sweetheart
Acting like he ain't have two babies

Denying their existence
Like wow this dude is crazy
He on that Mary J Blige stuff
"And it really messed me up"

Then you try to play me like I was the villain
But when it's time for your children to be tucked in at night
You were missing
Why are you up here treating your legacy
Like they have no feelings?

But when you got exposed...
The lengths that you went to cover it up was quite revealing
Don't text me to check in
Focus on the women you been screwing
Who have yet to figure out
About your baby mama and your children

Still Living

See I know you wanted me dead
Erase me from this world
And take my place instead
You waited so patiently
Played like you cared for me
Acted like we were friends

Tried to trick me into thinking
We were lovers
But darkness can't hide light
And light can never be covered for long

So I danced to your beat
I sung your song
Knowing you wanted me dead
I just thought if you knew how loving I was
I'd prove you wrong

But nothing changed
And your jealousy grew
Because you couldn't defeat me
And I wanted the best for you

Your Mama was devilish
And in so many words I told you so
Your dad ignored your pain
To start over and build a new family
And I remained silent
Out of respect for his lost

I watched your cousins steal from you

Over and over again
You treated the betrayal with smoke
You drank your heart stupid with gin

I told you that no drug could address toxic love
That your not willing to walk away from
But you looked at my exit as a slight
Turning against the only person that dared to stick around
That desired to hold you close
That dared to be down

So yeah, I knew you wanted me dead
These Chicago streets have damn near turned red
From people tryna save people
That want de head

But you can't fight demons
That people won't address
Thinking of ways to destroy you
Because the wicked receive no rest

If only we could go back to college
When your smile was brighter than the sun
Your future was ahead of you
And your hope was far from done

But you would rather kill me than see me rise
Because it's too painful to tackle
The evil you feel inside
So I'll send up a prayer for you

Deceitful

The heart of man is deceitful who can know it
But God
I keep tryna see the light in you
But damn you make it hard

Remember when your hatred came bubbling out
Because I was healed
But you were eager to uncover and reveal
My hidden trama

You love the drama
Where was your Mama to save me?
I'll never forget what you said,
Why are you so happy?
Remember when I used to touch you? Acting like you forgot!

When we were younger your hands were everywhere
I ran from them
Swung on you
And I fought you off with all the strength I could muster
I forgave you but it seems like forgiveness wasn't enough

I bet it ate you up
Like heaping hot coals on ya head
Because I'm living my life, free of condemnation
And your the walking dead

Why couldn't you just accept my kindness and run?
But, no. That's too much like right
You wanted me to be broken
Because you could never overcome

Yeah, you did what you did!
And it hurt
Because I was supposed to be able to trust you
You my kinfolk

But I choose to move on
Because ain't no pain strong enough to keep me shackled
When Christ came to set the captives free
I can already tell

Fresh on bail
And you're itching to pull out the worst in me
Don't make me break the 10 commandments
Thou shall not kill

Echoing in my head
Don't make me take a page from Celie?
I'll kill you Harpo
For I let you destroy me
Take your shattered conscious and leave
I don't think of you before I go to sleep

But you've brought havoc to so many lives
That I know
You'll never be able to stand toe to toe
With a sista like me

So no you can't borrow money
And no I am not scared
I am not your prisoner
And I will not succumb to the past
I chose to disregard

The heart of man is deceitful who can know it
But God
I keep tryna see the light in you
But damn you make it hard

Girl Child

Oh your so pretty
With manners too
Talk about polite
It obvious that your parents raised you right

Listen here:
Girl child,
Don't you talk too loud
Men don't like a woman yelling
And carrying on

Only lite words that reek of diet soda
Can come from your lips
And eat a little less
Watch your hips
You don't wanna gain too much weight

Don't ask questions only do as your told
Deny your spirit
Smother the needs of your soul
Act like a lady
Your words shouldn't be too bold
Unless you wanna live alone

Girl child,
Take small bites
Ignore the sound of your stomach growling
Hold your waist in
Keep your back straight
You don't wanna slouch on dates

A lady has to maintain
Even if your hairstyle is so tight
It squeezes your brain
You must not scratch

Hit it with some grease
And throw a bonnet on it
No matter what it feels like
You gotta flaunt it

Girl Child
Get in that hot kitchen
So you can know how to cook
Be able to make collard greens, cornbread and ham
Without referring to a southern cuisine book

You are beautiful to be sure
But put some concealer on
No one will talk to you
If your features are too strong

In other words, dampen your light
So that the less enlightened can shine
Society don't like a woman that's growing all the time
Settle for low job titles and substandard pay

That's what the status quo molds us to say
It refutes our right to think
Pressuring us to obey
And that reality is far from okay

Why not live a life with purpose?

We're not defined by the notions of yesterday
Hold your head up high
If you choose to be alone that's fine

Girl child,
Talk a little louder
So the people in the back can hear you
It's your time to be acknowledged
Your voice will sail with the breeze
It will get high like birds
Flying north after winter…

Removed From Facebook

This ain't my first rodeo,
I pack em up
I get em gone
What they know about a wild thing?

The ones that give songs bass
The hope that gives birds wings
I hit that drum
I ride the rhythm of tap, tap, tap

Crushing empty promises
That build false facades
When a person has no need to lie
Society treats them odd

You ran from the block
I lived on
Rather than act tough
God made me strong

I saw the bullets with no name
While you claim the hood I live in for street acclaim
You got the markings of a lame
I dated the thugs you ran from
And encouraged them to raise above the game

But up until now I never spoke on that
Because what's the use in talking about
Your ex's flipping crack
Catching yo dude hiding stacks

I'm the inspiration behind the masterpiece
Putting the battery in a lackluster back
Kick the mic stand for me
And bring it back with a bended knee

Meet me in the parking lot
A quarter past 3
When you with a real one
The truth always run deep
That's why people need me

For the grit they don't have
To stand as the rib that's missing
From perfectly chiseled abs
I wanna know

Can the church welcome a former pimp?
Can the congregation accept a hoe?
Till she don't wanna live that way no more
Praying for the brothers hustling outside the corner store

Pointing fingers and gossiping
Like your glass house is made of stone
The God of Abraham, Isaac and Jacob
That rose you to power watches from His throne

And has the ability to take away all the power you hold
I hear a lot of people talk
Like fat meat ain't greasy
Dealing with grief is hard
But listening to people gossip about your pain ain't easy

I mourned the passing of my Father, Auntie and Grandmother's death
In 9 months
So excuse me if I'm not a conversationalist
Don't take it personal if I'm blunt

But my struggle isn't the next man's lunch
Dine on your own problems
Dance on the bedrock of your own tears
The struggle my Father faced all his life

I dealt with for years
He ain't raise no marshmallows
In the darkness of the trenches
You dug for him
There was no help

He was security, advice giver,
Friend to the downtrodden
But he was looked down upon
By his own family because he had no earthly wealth

Rehabilitated hustler turned husband
I watched him be judged and demeaned
By those he lifted up
And defended to the end

Now tell me…
If you ever been a real one
How do you look at yourself?
You ignored the seeds planted in good soil
You spoke ill on the widow that stood ten toes down

Now watch Christ bless those you tried to break down
Don't call, don't text and don't back bite now
Just hold your peace as I hold my head high
I will dance on glistening water

My prayers will elevate higher than blue sky
I have worshiped in the valley
Praising while other people pass judgment
As I walk by
Save face for the sake of appearances

Remember what you told me at the private viewing
I should work hard to not become what people say about me
But that means little
Because I only care about what God says about me
That's why I removed y'all from Facebook

Being connected by blood
Doesn't make us close
Sometimes you're hurt
By the people you love the most

You got this all clotted up
For the survival of my heart
I have to thin out the herd
The feather passed around the flock
Is stripped from the birds

No more she said, he said, they said
But your respect of my situation remains silent
Everybody getting lifted off my story
And I didn't supply it

One mention of their cruelty
And them folks will start a riot
Even though you pay them no attention
They still gonna try you
Because in order for them to hide their hand
They have to deny you

But why stop there?
There was no simple road for me
Life provided no crystal stairs
I remember all the nights I went hungry
And family wasn't there
Friends looked on with pity but no one cared

So why bring up my affairs
You been assuming, talking and putting on airs
I don't profit from crying out woe is me
My pain has been coated with sunshine and gray skies
It's a mixture of ambiguity
But your methods are so cut and dry

My Dad told me not to give up
Or break down when he died
That's why I kept on going
Because he prepared me for the inevitable

He knew his time would come
He considered the survival of his family
Once his time on this side is done
Only you can decide what your legacy will be
But as for my Father, he was a real one
I always want my people to excel

Never wanted my kin folk to fail
Despite your cold shoulder and stale eyes
I pray for you still

No matter what you say about me just remember I love you still
But watch your mouth when you mention me
Because gossiping only causes division
And your contempt has left us divided
I prefer speaking directly to someone over secretly infighting
So let's talk about it

Silence

You deal with wickedness
For profit
Piling up evil doings in your dairy
Before you lock it

Remember when we sat on the couch
And I told you
Not to force drugs on her
I begged you to be kind

Staring at me through your scratched glasses
You blinked your eyes
You told me she would be let out the facility
But you made sure she died there

You wicked witch of the North
Was it necessary to silence her?
Did you think the truth wouldn't get out?
I see your indiscretions clear as day

You broke my heart
Brought bitter tears to my Mother's eyes
But in your arrogant indignation
You didn't care

I turned to God and begged for mercy
Please don't let my Grandma die this way!
Please I can't take it
I won't survive
I heard a peaceful voice reply, *I'm sorry*

The next night, I got a call from my Mother
Confirming that my Grandmother died
Shrouded in secrecy, decked out in lies
I know very little about her while she was alive

The person responsible for her death
Invited me to the funeral
A staged show
You killed the victim
Setup the burial
And expect me to go?
I said, *No. Let the dead bury the dead.*

I mourned at home doubled over in pain instead
Visions of our wrecked relationship swirled in my head
I know this is far from over
After everything you have done…
I wonder how you sleep at night?

Your pillow must be worn down
By the weight of your lies
Mother's day will come every year
As a reminder of the calamity you wrought

My world came crashing down for the third time
Because of your idle hands
Vomited for days on end
Vile things came up from my trembling body

This death left part of me dying
I thought of you…
And sighed

How could someone I've know all my life
Be so broken inside

You invited me to the funeral
A staged show
You killed the victim
Setup the burial
And expect me to go?
I said, *No. Let the dead bury the dead.*
For some reason I can't be mad at you
Even after what you did

A Poem About Mourning

There are no words
To fill the void
It is an endless sea
Of missed communication
And broken opportunities

How do I move forward?
How do I forget?
How do I cry?
Now that you're gone

Your things fill the room, storages and my mind
Vestiges of the life
You left behind
For the first time
You're not here to wipe my tears

They fill the rims of my dry eyes
Bubbling to the surface
Like a pop can
That was shaken and opened to soon

Where is your shoulder to cry on?
Where can one go to find your love?
The contour of your face
Was the comfort that tired consciences rested on

My Father, my friend, my rock has passed on
Jesus tell me who am I now?
Am I still his babygurl?
Or am I a fatherless child?

There are tangled gray wires
At the base of my swollen red heart
Unable to hold the contents
Of a soul torn apart

It pumps the same but it aches different
It pleads for a love far gone
Begging for attention in a world
That pays no mind

The mouth says, I'm well
Fingertips text, I'm fine
But deep down a stomach twisted in knots
Burns with a throbbing
That only the grieving know

How do I move forward?
How do I forget?
How do I cry?
Now that you're gone

When death darkens a humble doorstep
An unraveling spirit will gladly go home
Let the white picket fence fade into the background
Clouds hover in weightless air

They appear and disappear
As a glistening dawn opens
For those chained in the shackles of mourning
Morning after morning freed from the torment
Of a breaking heart that stays broke

Forgiveness

More precious than gold or silver
Valuable like rain in the desert
Drying out on the beach
Like seashells washed up on shore
It breaks under the pressure of bitterness
Eventually becoming fine sand
That gives way to happy, jogging feet
Eager to walk on to brighter days
Till time and heat transforms it to twinkling glass
Touched by the hand of time

Monster

I can feel you
Watching me from the deep
While I sleep
When I rise with crust in my eyes

You are pulling, pushing truth
An inalienable fact
Drawing lies from my lips
Putting sharp, precise daggers in my back

Remembering the mistakes I made
When I was 9 years old
Promising secrecy
But telling every cruel hearted thing you know

You inch around corners
Without making a sound
You have stolen riches and claimed crowns
Most people don't recognize your presence…
Until it's going down…
Jealousy is a green eyed monster indeed

You have taken love from innocent souls
Created pain that reverberates like an echo
Calling down empty corridors
For an open ear to receive
Pretending to love everyone
But your base is hate and envy

I see you moving like hard waves
Looking for a soft place to land

Maybe you'll stay in the ocean
Perhaps you will move to the sand

Either way… I will keep going forward
While you watch, I will progress…
Knocking down your house of cards
With ease and happiness!

Rise and Fall

Day

Says hello

It greets me

With sparkling warmth

I respond in kind

With anxious yawning

Daybreak shines in the morning

Cookout

Lip smacking can be heard across the street
Jovial voices saturated in' emboldened jubilee
Teeth locking onto the tender flesh of barbecued beef
Plaid patterned picnic tables are side by side

Topped with full pans of decadent soul food
Baked macaroni, roasted chicken, grilled beef polishes,
Hamburgers, potato salad and greens beans
Can be seen next to the red koolaid

The sugar that makes adults stay awake
Makes children misbehave
Long lost family show up to the gathering
In the newest fits and the hottest kicks

Every ounce of blemish is covered by bronzer
And foundation made by Maybelline
There is an open bar full of gin and tonic
It tastes good but it's affects are toxic

After hours of dancing and conversations galore
Drunk people stumble away from the party floor
But as soon as they reach the door
They are questioned about their way home…

Who is driving? Are they sober?
If not, we finding someone to drive ya'll there
We want y'all to be safe because we care.
Just tell Juju the location
And he'll take you there
We all family here!

Ice Numbs It

It's a small truth, I rarely discuss
I'm turned on by love
And seduced by lust
Still I get upset when sweet kisses don't stay

When betrayal is my bitter water
And lies my meal of the day
But it's hard for me to turn you away
So I try to downplay it

Because I don't want people to know…
That deep down I'm hurt
And reeling as a result of being emotional
How do I deal with feelings
My heart can't control?

When all I ever wanted
Was to be cared for by you
Now I have a slow ache
In the place where my heart used to be

All alone in my kitchen
Surrounded by food
But I can't eat!
My appetite has been taken from me

Yet ice cream tastes good
Even when I'm in the midst of sadness
One thing is understood…
Ice numbs the pain.

Yet to See

Your love is sweet sunshine on a rainy day
It speaks to dormant souls
Bringing hope to the surface like condensation
On a glass of cold lemonade

Your love is cool shade in the scorching heat
It is easy to feel alive and bask under your tree
The eggs that cooked on the sidewalk
Are scrambled from the trampling of our busy feet

We are poetry in motion
A small boat in a big ocean
Our love goes deep, it sails wide
Always wondering if it will reach the otherside

That is the nature of what we have
It is too good to feel bad
We move to the rhythm of laughter
Smiling with the happiness embedded in our hearts

No power but death can come between
And no man on God's green earth can tear us apart
We scurry to the finish line with unspoken desire
And gold ambition in our quivering hands

Without apprehension we make our stand
To care for each other unconditionally
In the midst of a broken and dismal land
Believing in a reality we have yet to see

I waited for the break of aging time

But wrinkles never formed on the hands
And rust never touched the dial
Meanwhile, I moved eagerly to the sound of tic toc tic
My arms stretched out like eagle wings ready to soar
My feet stepped in sequence to the beat of unrealized dreams

Deadlines have evaded me
Pit stops have kept me sidetracked too long
I begged and pleaded for a moment
That surpassed my meager understanding
Patience is not on my side
But I nurture it with hope birthed in the belly of my soul

Awaiting a season that beckons the seed
That laid dormant in harsh winters
And endured the bitter rain of a spring not quite broken
That sat through the abundantly hot weather of summer
Only to arrive at fall all over again

Do not let the time of harvest past me
Let my crops rise up strong from barren, decrepit soil
The foundation is hard but my ground is solid
The wind may blow but my bedrock will not giveaway
The sound of steady brass ticking
Fills my heart with anticipation

Everyday is another chance to face my struggles and grow
No amount of daylight savings can stop the progress I have made
I am claiming my tomorrow today!
There is no biological clock bigger than my aspirations
I will live with the sunshine on my face
And the darkness on my back

Standing in the truth
That is awaiting those who smile in the midst of adversity
Now and forever my heart will sing a new song
I will sit near the edge of the dock awaiting the breath of daybreak
Soon my seeds will blossom
And I will dance upon the ease of their arrival

Their leaves will open like unraveling scrolls of truth,
Not yet realized
But ready to exist in the cool breeze of Monday mornings
Awaiting the warm feeling of resting dew drops
Time has taught me patience
Because the greatest things in this life
Aren't acquired easily

Never the Same

I look to you
And the icy dreams of your warm embrace
Aching to feel the smooth contours of a chiseled face
Your presence is a sweet melody to me

Reminding a lonely soul of treasured memories
Let love swing from misty air like dandelion spores
Just one blow of cool breeze
Could sweep all of my desires away

But every time I'm gone too long…
You beg me to stay
I dare not ask you where you've been
Because I have no answer for myself

The joy is short lived
But we settle for brief moments
Until it's put back on the shelf
Running back and forth between fading lines

Wondering if the truth is valued
Finding a tragic yet seductive nuance in a lie
We have a connection, you and I
That turns blue skies gray

Kiss me 50 times as my troubles fade away
Chasing after the bliss
While forgetting the challenges of yesterday
Hoping we'll stay together

But knowing some things can never be the same

I still look to you
Throwing empty promises at a decrepit dream
That may never come true

Restless

I dream of you in midday
With no shadows in sight
You are my getaway
You make my world feel right
So whenever you're away...
I expect restless nights

Rewind

Bring it back
So we can see it in slow motion
Let's watch it again
Don't let the tape keep going

It moves too fast
The best scenes are sorely missed
Skipping like a record stuck on repeat
The silver of it reflects like a mirror

Blurred horizontal lines
That flash and blink in discontent unison
Are followed by appalling noises
That appear on the tube
Someone yells, *the VCR is on the fritz again*

So it does little to lighten up the room
Take it out
Wipe it off
Then press play

We all gather round
For the antics played out on TV
Wanting to relive the moment just one more time
How many times can we press rewind?

The remote wasn't ready for the pressure applied
But the buttons were pushed anyway
The oil of eager fingertips rubbed off the characters
And the plastic was no match for incessant rewinding

The challenge was met every night
Fighting against the normalcy
Of running a feature film without interruption
Until one day, the triple A batteries died
And the battle was lost

But once the remote was restored
We went back to business as usual
Telling people to stop talking over the movie
Pausing and running out for a much needed bathroom break
Only to realize that we have to rewind

It moves too fast
The best scenes are sorely missed
Skipping like a record stuck on repeat
The silver of it reflects like a mirror

It is lodged in the 90s
Like orange Hi-C, digital pets and aol internet discs
This we record
Moments like this are hard to forget
So we rewind

Part 3

Feed The Soul

One thing about love,
Either it is or it isn't.
There are no in-betweens.

People

Some people don't care about people
But it's deeper than what you think
Lost in a sea of…
What do they mean to me?
They are alone surrounded by people
Who fail to comprehend…
What is a lover, family member or friend?

Everyday is poker
At night it's russian roulette
Who will mistake me for a kind person?
Then I use them till there's nothing left?
Run up their patience and love
Leaving their heart in debt

The problem that affects me, you and you
It starts with the iphone, ipad and love of "I"
What about the hurt the next person feels inside?
When we focus only on our ambitions
Trying to gain investors to keep retention
But we care little for the person were selling to

Some people don't care about people
But it's deeper than what you think
Lost in a sea of what can they do for me?
They are alone surrounded by people
Who fail to comprehend…
What is a lover, family member or friend?

Emptiness fills an empty chest
But we lie and testify that we're blessed

Calling on the name of Jesus
With our hands held high
Bearing false witness for passers by

Only feening, got pride
No desire to love without conditions
Causing pain to others but never paying attention
Expecting something different but getting a similar rendition

Sometimes I don't care about people
But it's deeper than what you think
I've had people trying destroy me since I was 14
Classmates, school officials, family too
For some I was a friend
But others treated me like a tool
It's the type of pain no one should get use too

So I watch my back
One minute someone claims to be my lover
Next they're trying to attack
Why is it so hard to show affection
And receive it back?

In the distance is a heart ready to love
And a sea of forgiveness
Deep enough to fit all of us
If only we realized it's deeper than what we we think
We would care a little more
Without wanting something in return

A warm smile will do
Anonymous virtue is fine

But in this capitalistic society
Everyone is injured and looking for the bottomline

In Your Shell

Do you like your shell?
I know that it's full of unused space
Does the opaque color make you feel at ease?
Unable to recognize your ever evolving face

But I know your cold
Tired of swapping shells
Because you're in need of a cozy home
You glide and crawl through darkness

Scared to move in the open space alone
But never willing to open up
To anyone other than yourself
So all your self-worth, secrets and wealth
Is stashed in a small crawl space

Your decorative outside
Dazzles the unsuspecting eye
But its a cover all the same
A place to run, a dwelling to duck,

Coverage from the cold rain
A mollusk depraved of uninhibited freedom
As you move slowly through life
With no direction at all

Seeking happiness that always stalls
Staggering to touch a love that never calls
So I will ask you again…
Do you like your shell?

Lighthouse

I admit I'm not the same women in the Polaroids anymore
I had to change to survive
To hold onto to the light that I thought had died

I spent time fighting to survive
Every note I sung off-key
Every quiet moment
Full of contemplation and maybes

I still fill up my mind with thoughts of you
Wondering if you're okay?
Questioning if you have someone new?
I thought I would go through the trials and tribulations of life with you

But I had to do it alone
Away from everything I knew, only to change and grow
I checked out
Like the dark spots in between the lights on a freeway
Looking for traces of you along the way

I needed to know you were there
Even if I never heard from you at all
Everyday in the silent recesses of my mind
I wanted you to call

But you waited on me to reach out instead
Pride has left us without us
Looking at you sideways knowing deep down
You're the only person I can trust

Sometimes I wonder why you?
Why not someone new?
Why does my heart call for you like a lighthouse?
Calling a boat to shore
Watch out for the rocks and jagged edges?
As I shine my light for you

There's more to me than you know
I have pain undisclosed, never fixed and left uneven from years ago
But my eyes are the same
My heart is the same
My hope is the same

I got used to hiding the brightness of my flame
But I admit
I'm not the same woman in the polaroids anymore
I had to change to survive
To hold onto the light that I thought had died

Pools

Can I love you with my eyes closed?
Just ease into the comfort of your embrace
As I imagine you staring at the contours of my face
Feeling every second as though it were my last

Thinking nothing of the future
And neglecting the mistakes of the past
Falling in love with the thought of loving you more
Wondering what two people so enamored
With each other even argued for?

It's the bridge of your nose that does it for me
The way it rises and falls when you tilt your head
The shape of your almond eyes
The length of your legs
The connection I feel to the palm of your hands
When they grip mine

Even when I don't speak to you
I think about you all the time
Can I love you with my eyes closed?
Just ease into the comfort of your embrace
As I imagine you staring at the contours of my face

Feeling every second as though it were my last
And even when we're not together
I close my eyes and I think about how I love you still
Always have and always will

Our love is like ice that freezes in winter
And thaws in spring

You'd be surprised by the change a season can bring
I will wait for you at the door of summer
When our love has turned into a vibrant lake
So I can swim in the pools of your eyes once more

Missing Rubber Bands

Can we dream here underneath a copper moon?
The fireflies move in and out of darkened spaces
While buzzing near familiar faces
Only to be captured in jars by children
Seeking to bring the light a bit closer

Till at last they are set free to roam the land
When the sun falls behind the rolling hills of resting prayers
But you will see them again
They move with the breeze
They live in the wind

Freedom sings lullabies to aged responsive ears:
Wade in the water
Wade in the water children
Wade in the water
God's gonna trouble the water

Knees covered in mud and agony
Can not stop the journey
That began in the hearts of man
Inching toward a grander tomorrow than the one seen today

Reaching out for love
But receiving hate in return
Loose ends of failed equity unravel
Like braided hair unsealed by rubber bands

The children mature into adults
The wounds fade
But the desire to preserve is here to stay

Clawing for a chance to move beyond the struggles of yesterday
To grab hold of the copper moon
While chasing fireflies

Stronger

Giants fell here
Leaving rumble, desolate land and overflowing seas
Man has searched 1,000's of years
For the perfect ecstasy

Only to find that the high
Comes down
Because even it is subject to gravity
The liquor wears off
The dreams stumble into restlessness

The lovely song
Stops its incessant melody
We are love
Everyone of us

Created and baked into perfection with care
It matters not
If your Father, Mother, Auntie, Uncle
Or friends were there

I'm sure you've heard
Absence makes the heart grow fonder
Well I believe
Absence makes the heart grow stronger

Lust

He calls me on the phone
But he don't call me
He speaks to lust
And the desire for an opportunity

Begging and pleading
Calls turn to bellows
Like a stoned cat
With no back alley to walk

He lurks for me
Drunk in the moonlight
With the compulsion to stalk
Hiding, waiting to pounce

Feeling that he owns
What belongs to me
Days followed by empty nights
Chasing down maybes
But he don't call me

Love

Write on my heart
Tales of hope
Moments of lost and found
A journal with missing entries
A notebook unbound

Scribble your thoughts and dreams
With a airplane in the sky
As eager eyes await a new sunrise
Jot down the words you can't describe
Write a love letter
That will pass from hand to hand
And never die!

Quench a roaring fire
Our ambitions will soar like kites
We can't get much higher
Let your words run like midnight trains
With no station in sight

You can see in the day
But you can only feel at night!
You are twilight splintered over dawn
With soft hope enticing me
The swoops and curves of your fingerprints

And a burgeoning horizon to sit on
I await on your arrival like a letter in the mail
But will think of you
Even when your long gone
Because you are written on my heart

Evening

Evening says, *Goodnight*
It welcomes me with a cool breeze
Where shadows bounce off the bark
Of easing going trees

It speaks in riddles
But is majestic like noon day
Some people love the night
Nocturnal souls come out to play

The owl hoots
The bat screeches
The tired snore
But when all is done
The rising sun comes out once more

Missing you

Incoherent whispers fall on wayward ears
And are broken on jagged rocks
Where are you when I need you?
Flutters…
In the distance

The Past

It bears no consequence
There is more to life
Than the pain that lies behind quiet tears
There is no brokenness here

The turbulence you have seen
Happiness that has gone to rot
You are the newness
That grows in the place of the old

Like wet honey dripping off the comb
Too fresh to be packed away
Too wild to be sold
Made to be unique
Born to be bold

You are the beginning of a hatching story
Waiting to be told
So the past…
Matters not

Ode to Laughter

My stomach is in knots
My esophagus goes into shock
This conversation is boiling hot
With laughter

Little did I know
5 minutes ago
Smiles would break disappointed faces
Hope would change the room

Like a good book forever turning pages
Conversation goes on for miles
Glistening teeth and funny phrases
Jokes that come off as outrageous

Giggling that spreads like wildfire
Because it's contagious
Oh laughter
How precious you are to me

What About Love?

It's easy to fixate on the struggle
Focus on your hustle
When complicated feelings get involved
Is it possible to love someone
Without being prepared to fall?

Terrified of facing a truth
That can't be covered
Diving but unable to swim in deep water
Drowning in desire and conflicted

Searching for an everlasting kiss
That doesn't disappear in the morning like mist
To love, to care, to push, to reminisce
To acknowledge, to strive, to hope, to survive
To do more than live an empty life

We must embrace the feeling of intimacy
To be close
To breath in the fragrances of bitter wine
To grab a hand and be held in sunshine

If only for a moment that stands still
Whether it be by accident or will
We hold on…
To the feeling of love

Dust

We're here one day
And gone the next
Like particles of dust
Being blown around
From sunrise to dusk
We grow old but never rust
That's the special thing about us

Someone Else

It pains my heart to see you with another
To take in the breath of her smile
To lounge in the comfort of a long embrace
To rest easy and be at peace for a little while

My love was once enough for you
The light of your eyes meeting mine
Was our beginning
The rough contours of your large hands held mine like secrets

We swayed on still yet lively water
Our kisses took air that couldn't be replaced
Only recycled and started a new
I turned my face from your countenance
But I loved everything about you

Your skin like rich melting chocolate
Left in heat too long
A lion's mane of unmitigated disaster
That grew long and strong
Every dark, course powerful coil leading to another

Talk to me
Turn phrases into words my imagination dreamed of
But never heard
Let your voice fly over distant skies like a hummingbird

Talk to me once more
Our love has shattered like a china plate
But the sound of the breaking
Was worth waiting for

Never Apart

Glistening truth
Rest easy on my hand
Caress my face
Speak to my chilly soul

Unthawing frozen feelings
With hopeful resolve
We sit together
Taking in the scenery

Laughing like old friends
Reunited at summer's end
Sunglasses utilized for your presence
A bright smile illuminates my heart

Millions of miles
Have stood between us
But I see you from a distance
So it feels like we were never apart

To be closer to the sun
To feel that something new has begun
Spending afternoons
Taking in your rays of light

Something Different

I don't wanna be that bitter soul…
Mad at my exes
Judging someone else
But never looking at my imperfections

I point my blame in another direction
Running from the truth…
Scared to make a confession
I wanna be the person that grows
From hard learned lessons

Like a rose blooming
In the midst of rumble and concrete
My mistakes were many
Tryna survive in these streets
While being quiet and meek

I learned plenty
I rolled up the blunt, smoked it
Then hit the henny
Didn't want no food

So I drunk wine that was my life
For years at a time
I soaked my pillow
With the tears of a broken heart

I changed along the way
I lost my faith
I broke up and broke down
And lost my way

I fell into the traps
Hurt myself
And stared at the ocean
From the dock of the bay
"Wasting time…"

But I stand here today
Free at last
The remnants of a painful past
No longer hold me

I have gone beyond the fear
Of being the old me
I walk with Christ
Laying in his bosom
Is comfort for me

I don't have to run to man or parties
I don't have to be the prettiest in the room
The person always trying to be super attractive
But they peaked too soon

Looking for confirmations
In likes and affirmations
Living in a world where many believe they are free
But never received emancipation

The shackles begin in your mind
It was the first time
Someone told you what you couldn't achieve
Because of the color of your skin

You became a beautiful bird
With a broken leg living in a gilded cage
Would you fly free if someone opened the door?
Or is flying free too big of a chance?

Many of us are afraid of soaring
A fear of being struck out the sky
What if our desires are too high?
What if you never try?
Then you never know

Then it all boils down to, *Oh well*
That was me till I woke up in hell
Removed from walking the boulevard of broken dreams
I had time to reflect on my feelings

"Why don't I feel like I'm good enough?"
The thoughts I allowed to penetrate my mind
Words reverberating like,
"Your cute for a dark skin girl but you'll never be fine"

I accepted things… I should of denounced
I allowed bitterness into my house
But it's a new season
It's time to dust the cobwebs out

When you're built on a good foundation
A strong wind won't take you
Opinions won't sway you
A flood won't wash you away

You were made for a time such as this

To create in a time
Where creativity is not important if you look good
But why should it matter?

Some people believe happiness will come
When their butt is fatter
Others when their hair is down their back
Or if their playing people like chess

It would be better
If love rained from the sky
And we'd all feel better inside
No need to run, unable to hide

A cease fire on the war of the sexes
By forgiving ourselves
Those who hurt us and our exes
We can walk in a new direction
And do something different

Part 4

Happiness in Transition

Thoughts move
A mile per minute
Tangling themselves around little things
That equal up to nothing in the end
Electric pulses lighting up
With every neuron fired
A new idea is birthed

Speak

Talk to me like words are all you have left
If you don't kiss me soon
Young lungs will run out of breath
Talk to me like running water
Pouring out
From hidden streams
Conversation turned fantasy
Living in the oasis of an unknown dream
When you speak to me

Profit

You my dear
Are bold like red wine
Bitter like sour grapes
Robust like the aroma of coffee
Sailing from the pot into your senses

You are strong like a bull
Powerful like the black coat of an ox
Dangerous like a sharp pen
That only speaks truth

You move like wind through
Swift trees
But your smile speaks like
Naivety sprung in youth

You put it on em
When they question your authenticity
Never afraid to get in the kitchen
And bake Grandma's old recipes

Them smothered fried pork chops
Fried chicken and macaroni
That encourages the soul
You are the rose that bloomed from concrete

A tinder heart
That opted for something better than the streets
That fought to be something other than a statistic
You prey on weak minds

Coming for blood
Eager for plugs like tampons left behind
Flushed to a land before time
A truth born without reason or rhyme

Pushed out of childhood before season
Tryna make it in a society that crushes dreams
Being offered temptation
Like diamonds and pearls
What does it profit a person
To gain the world and lose their soul

Able to Find

Logic has failed to explain you
Are you the quiet after the storm
The prayer before a large meal
The glue holding a fragile heart together
The heat that melts blue steel

What are you indeed
Maybe you're a rubik's cube
In an unsteady hand
Or a balance beam
One uneasy step and I'm falling
With no safe place to land

Could you comfort an empty stomach?
Like soul food on thanksgiving
The body is enticed
But the heart is unwilling
Holding on to pieces that glue couldn't hold together

Easing into soft cushions
And kind thoughts
Searching for open crevices
And hopes that a broken soul forgot

Tender kisses and sweet words
Hidden oasis,
Wrapped around action and inaction
Caught up in metaphors and verbs

We pause
Go

Proceed
Rewind

In the day
The sky is yours
At night
Thoughts of me take up your time

Living in a day dream
While focusing on the sublime
Working towards a reality
That few are able to find

Telephone

He is looking for a place
That's safe to go
Where love flows from streams
And passion explodes from anxious hope

Carrying a weary head in need of a pillow
Or a place where he can lay his burdens down
And rest his strained soul
Enabling happiness to grow

His cousin told his uncle
Who relayed the word to his mother
That then passed it on
To a great Auntie that didn't know

Sweltering Heat

Spicy words taste like Tabasco dreams
Speak jalapeno to me
Like cayenne peppers blowing back sweltering heat
Speak sriracha to me

Like hot sauce mixed with red chilies and vinegar
Desiring a feeling of numb lips
Brought on by scorching roof
You can never be hotter than the searing sun

It shines for the world but bows to the Son
Yet I look toward the zesty flavor
Which burns with the fiery and passion of words spoken
With a hint of sizzling mustard sauce

It can not be cooled down by milk
It's fire is tangy
Ignited by the truth of the Holy Ghost
Clearing the pathway to closed doors

Giving light to dark spaces
Changing the temperature and atmosphere
That's why I like heat
Speak sriracha to me

Much Needed Rest

Take me to your island
Where I can bask in the sweet sun
Swing in the night breeze
And frolic until my work is done

Just breath easy
No expectation for the anticipation
Of conversation
In truth, I want to rest

Experience joy, peace and happiness
No hurt in my voice
No ache in my chest
An end to the shakiness of breath

Where is the curve in the rainbow
Does it wait for me?
In the midst of this craziness
Can a misunderstood soul
Discover a bedrock of tranquility?

Sleep anxious body
Lay down your nervous flesh
You've held on long enough
Too tired to be emotional
Too emotional to be tough

So take me to your island
Where I can bask in the sweet sun
Swing in the night breeze
And frolic until my work is done

Twist and turn on a path outlined by cleared foliage
It leads through the bush
To a shoreline that sore soles need
Play in the warm sand

Dip excited toes in refreshing water
Afterward laugh and smile
Forget my troubles for a little while
This is my day to be free
Live with comfort
Wind down with ease

The ebb and flow of palm trees is a sight to behold
They gave pause to a worried mind
And silence to a complex feeling
Their leaves shift from side to side
Yet the bark stands tall

Late Bloomer

Happiness painted her face
Giving form to shapeless dreams
Dull lines illuminated with the glow of sunshine
Devoid of harsh rays

A twinkle sparkles and dances
In the center of black pupils that were once cold
Now when she speaks the room stops and listens
Because her words have meaning
They are spoken with intention

The bulb that no one ever thought would bloom has blossomed
Into a rose with vibrance and color
It grew free from pruning
The change came with no stress

Just the embrace of new days dawning
Coated in the feel of happiness, without onlookers it grew
Into a flower no one expected
Into a beautiful decadence that made easy days feel brand new

It stands alone surrounded in a bush by others
Because it has the sweetest fragrance
The splendor of it's petals have curb appeal
It beckons to the spiritually needy

It inches closer to bees which land and sit still
A moment to gather pollen will come
After a short rest
Here thoughts can be collected

As peace in an ever changing world holds more sway
It treasures the time spent with ease
And after a much needed nap
It will seize the day

She provides sweet morning dew for the thirsty traveler
Then sends them on their way
You became a pitstop for the restless souls
Seeking a safe place to go and lay their burdens down

Skin

This flesh,
My flesh is soft, succulent and brown
A hue passed down
From my Grandpappy

It's moisture maintained by shea butter
These are the lips
That gave sweet dreams to dry eyes
Full and shiny like the sunrise

Hands that cradled
Water from many streams
Used to toil, eager to clean
These are the fingers

That knitted woven things
This flesh,
My flesh is soft, succulent and brown
A hue passed down

From my Grandpappy
But sometimes it betrays me
Cute can turn angry with no food
It cries out:

Feed me before I turn rude
Always wanting what it can't have
Trading in the desires of the heart
For all the shortcuts that make the spirit sad
It specializes in hiding the good
Within a shell of bad

Elastic
Like a rubber band
It snaps back
Tighter than spandex jeans

But when wrinkles do come…
My skin will wear it
As a badge of honor
Come and see

The signs of a life well lived
Look at the temple that gave
And still gives
This flesh is my flesh
And it is what it is

New Day

I let you grow
Till I changed
I let you be free
Till a new day came

And when it arrived…
I cradled your tethered strands
In cuffed hands
The shells and metal beads detached
Till warm November came
And I burned the hair and memories to ash

To be fresh and short
Cut and dyed
Fried and parted to the side
Is a tale of an old scalp becoming new

I found death between these strands
Yet I'd be a lair if I said, I didn't miss you
Much like a car coming to a fork in the road
We must separate

I let you grow
Till I changed
I let you be free
Till a new day came

Descent

The night falls like a blanket
But we run away from it
Sure that it will catch our coattails
In its descent
But we keep going anyway

Rock Steady

I want that rock steady love
What you doing?
What you thinking of?
Type of love

The feeling that you crave
Reminiscent of stars shining from above
Drenched in the cover of twilight
And grinning smiles

You make my midnight bliss
You make my morning worth while
I'm gonna love you like vinyl records
It's never going out of style

I'm going to hold you
Like the seashore riding the waters edge
We make waves without even trying
But as we grow close, we pull away

We're a hop, skip and jump away like the Virgin Islands
Throw a rope laced with hope
So our worlds can collide
We talk easy, act greasy but we're bubbly on the inside

Some call it love others call it life
We play it cool
Like cold drinks splashed over ice
We don't always agree
But when we're together it feels right

Love Jones

I seen some rugged nights
Stuck in a desert storm
Where few things felt right
Looking for tears
But my eyes found none insight

The banks were empty
And the wells ran dry
The cactus pricked my finger
I crumbled inside
I was once a green, radiant thing
But it's been a long time since I felt alive

Sand covered my hopes
Like a rose encased in glass
I wanna believe in something more
That love much like a kiss
Is an opening door

That touching and being held in a warm
embrace is something
Worth trying for
To be smitten
To be tied up in the moment
To be adored

To be an object of affection
But not objectified
To feel kindness and tenderness
My heart was once denied
It's like a prayer in the night reaching God's ear

From my reality and becoming real
I've done so much
Hoping for a relationship where I can feel safe
Yet and still... Indulging in intimacy
That ignites a light inside

Every intrigue that I thought had died
It's something about your eyes
When they link up with mine
It's as though a tango were happening
In and out of time

Caught up in the rapture of love
That feels sublime
Most women wanna make love to your body
I'm tryna stroke your mind
Have you ever had a poet speak
Sweet nothings in your ear

Grab ahold of your day dreams
And tell you all the things you'd never hear
Get wrapped up in my stanzas
Listen to the beating of your heart
While my words draw you near

Is my pen true?
Does it bleed to speak of the things,
People and places
That I once knew?
But even in the midst of those scribbles
The blue lines in-between call for you
To desire your lips

All the passion that I rather ignore
Because I'm shocked that it's exists

To desire your hands entangled in mine
To feel the weight of your body against my hips
This could be the start of something of beautiful
You could be my love jones

Travel With Hope

Ride on
Move forward
Traverse to destinations unseen
Only experienced in dreams

Inch closer to the desires
Placed in your heart
Push through valleys
Pedal up mountaintops
Thrive in the midst of the wilderness

Sail over running rapids
As robust waterways swell
Let the dirt road
Build the level of your endurance

The challenge will make you reach higher
The time spent fighting will make you travel lighter
Because smooth highways
And byways are meant for driving

But it is the difficult terrain that builds us
Shaping our hard days
Into faith and trust
Creating a spirit that can withstand
The journey in no man's land

Race

You were made to cross powerful rivers
The tide will quell at your feet
Your chill will extinguish a volcano
In the midst of erupting

The wind of your hand will break barriers
That bar your entrance
Doors will swing open
When you turn about face

You are special with a presence
That can't be replaced
So when you are being challenged
Move like you already won the race!

Eagle

Bright green grass bends with ease and grace
Latching on to the qualms of the day
Swaying with the embrace of the wind
Cool desires drench happy blades

The brown, hard soil cracks underfoot
Meanwhile, aged, off-white feathers grip the open air
Catching the warmth of endless sunlight
Boundaries melt away here

Let the blue sky spread out before you
Scale the height of it
Take in the baby blue majesty
Live in the moment
Shape your body effortlessly to flow in it

Feel the passive breath lifting you higher and higher
Now is the beginning of a new tomorrow
Live for today
Plan for the future you are unable to see

Be eager in flight
Sailing and soaring to unseen destinations
In territories that curious souls dare to know
Faith will take you to places
That fear never will

Think of You

How many times
I come up short doesn't matter
As long as I keep pushing
Armed with the determination
To win

I struggle, fumble the ball
Left feeling worthless
With no self esteem to speak of
But I stand tall

When the road gets rigid, rocky and unbearable
I think of you
I wonder what would you do
To make it through
And I try again

You are valuable
Every hair on your head counted
All your triumphs and failures dearly noted
The black charcoal will soon turn into a diamond

When pressure is applied
The shine of it will reflect off of dim places
Creating a light where none existed
You are the bright twinkle in the distance

Showing from a far
Signaling the lost and the downtrodden
To a place and a person
That is willing to hear them

Your prayers stand in the gap for many
A friend to those
Who never had any person that cared
You are welcoming
Because your smile is always there

It checks on people and reassures them
That everything will be okay
Your eyes relate the truth with simple glances
Giving people hope for second chances
When you speak to others
And show concern for their well-being

Relating respect and kindness from the beginning
No matter the struggle
You find a way to be supportive
Being a blessing to others in their time of need
You are a child of the King
Jesus died so you could live more abundantly

Lasting Love

May God meet you where anguish starts
Where your burdens are heavy
And you look for the beginning and the end
Of your broken heart

You may suffer but your tears have courage
You may fall but your spirit will stand
You may struggle to comprehend
You may fail to understand

But you have the breath of life in your lungs
You have the making of victory in your hands
Glory is found in the valley of your despair
But your breakthrough is there in the dry land

Because the low place will take you to the mountain top
We can't see the future
But we know His mercy
And grace will endure

Carefully Made Home

Build your home on a solid foundation
One that surpasses shaky, uneven sand
Because a dwelling fixed on stable ground
Is made to stand

So when the wind blows, the rain falls
Impending flood waters come
And the sparse earth trembles
Your walls will endure

When the march of uncertainty comes like a storm
You can sit in your house fortified by good bones
After spending a lifetime paying it off
It's something that your children will own

They will sit in your old rocking chair
And get teary eyed and stare off into the distance
Remembering their adolescence in that home
Something created on solid soil
Based in treasured memories

My Truth

I'm a poet's poet
To hear it
Breath it
Relish in the truth
And know it

I'm a get yo butt in the house
Before the street lights come on
Baby, I'm a you think you wild
I'm gonna show you crazy

I'm a big mama in the church pew,
Stop snoring before I pinch you child
You know I come from dat easy bake oven,
Playing freeze tag, acting wild

Barrette's and bobo's on hair
Dancing with a mop
Using a brush as a mic type
I'm that schoolhouse rock
Loli loli loli minus Lil Wayne

First kiss with the entrance of spring
And all the confusion that new love brings
Playing house
And imaging a life with finer things

I'm a poet's poet
To hear it
Breath it
To relish in the truth

And know it

I decided to get saved
Because I needed a love that was everlasting
I want someone to die for me
The way Christ died for His passion

Give me some southern ice tea
In a rocking chair on a porch
In the middle of nowhere
So I can watch the clouds go by

As I wonder how black birds get so fly
Dazing off into a feeling of elevation
As I watch the sky
Open spaces, devoid of the faces
And places I know

I'm a dreamer
Missing sleep, no z's, low on sheep
I stay awake at night
And search deep

I'm a poet's poet
To hear it
Breath it
To relish in the truth
And know it

Even when the bottom fall out these shoes
I'm not folding
I'm like a brown cadillac on 4 flats

No air in the tires
But still gonna keep on rolling

See most people
Never sailed in a room full of vultures
Smile a little bit
But still keep a cold shoulder

Utilize discretion
Be nice but not too nice
Comrades can be flipped
If the price is right

I'm a poet's poet
To hear it
Breath it
To relish in the truth
And know it

Material World

I am convinced
Totally and utterly convinced
That everybody wants to be special to somebody
To look at someone with loving eyes
And to see love staring back at you

To feel the warm
And giving nature
Of an open palm
Pressing into the depths of a hand
Dying to be held

Love is ever changing like water
It exists and moves with no sense of time
We dedicate books, sonnets, movies
Portraits, paintings, songs, shows of affection
To the blossoming beauty of a love everlasting
That knows no bounds

And the very thought of someone caring for you
No matter your age
Is enough to bring joyful tears to weary eyes
The shared feelings of mutual respect, comradery
And trust is very special indeed

You see
We need each other
To have and to hold
Till breath breathes no more
And tales of gallantry and triumph grow old

We stand united
Connected by a burning eternal fire
That will rage in our heart
When every other light is nowhere to be found
You are bound to a cause greater
Than loving the material world
When we choose to love each other

New Beginnings

Rivers pour into closed rooms
That never expected to be filled
The mind is doing fine
But the soul is running

It's gone off pills
Chasing after fool's gold
That sprang forth from eroded morals
And long forgotten character

You use to love for the sake of love
You use to care with bear hugs
And desperate eyes
That pleaded for eloquent and truthful kisses

Wrapped in a cocoon of sweet lies
In a wicked world
We can never find joy in needful things
Iced out chains, foreign cars and diamond rings

Whatever happened to long walks in the park?
Getting soaked in the falling rain
Talking on the phone
Till the sky turns from light to dark

To touch someone's spirit and to ensnare their heart
To desire that part
Folding into each other's arms
Like warm laundry on a sunday morning

Every crease takes on new meaning

And leads to another
That rests in the corners of your smile
Connected to the web of your hand

To meet the sunrise on hot, brown sand
Saying that you'll never love
Only to love once again
Today is where a new beginning begins

A Few Words for the Road

Don't worry about the plans that fell through. Better things lie ahead of you. The ants don't worry about approaching boots on the ground. They keep working. Carrying crumbs twenty times their weight. Securing the hill they must maintain. Much like the small yet determined ants you must keep going. The closed doors stop short of rejection. They are a turning point in a long journey that you started with little help from friends and lots of prayer. Never feel that your efforts and your struggle are in vain.

The creation of this book was by no means a small undertaking. At every turn, I found myself looking for the courage to write what's in my heart as opposed to relying on the creativity stored in my soul. It was only later that I discovered they are two halves of the same whole. Together their abilities are limitless but separated they are powerless to stir the bastion of hope that lives in each and every one of us. Thank you for reading!

Love always, Esha

Notes

www.ingramcontent.com/pod-product-compliance
Lightning Source LLC
Chambersburg PA
CBHW051654040426
42446CB00009B/1134